For

Bonnie
From Jan
1994

OLD AGE
is not for
SISSIES

A Witty Look At Aging

Compiled by
Lois L. Kaufman

With illustrations by
Lyn Peal Rice

PETER PAUPER PRESS, INC.
WHITE PLAINS · NEW YORK

Copyright © 1989
Peter Pauper Press, Inc.
202 Mamaroneck Avenue
White Plains, N.Y. 10601
ISBN 0-88088-454-1
Library of Congress No. 88-63465
Printed in Singapore
7 6 5

Age isn't important unless you're cheese.

I don't want to achieve immortality through my work. I want to achieve it by not dying.

Woody Allen

About the only thing that comes to us without effort is old age.

Middle age is when everything starts to wear out, fall out or spread out.

Old age is when you can't remember what you never forget.

Old age is when your wants turn into wents.

If you're pushing 50, that's exercise
enough.

Women are not forgiven for aging. Bob
Redford's lines of distinction are my old-
age wrinkles.

Jane Fonda

The reports of my death are greatly
exaggerated.

Mark Twain

You know you're getting older when you
do the crossword puzzle in ink because
you can't read the answers in pencil.

Age is a high price to pay for maturity.

Tom Stoppard

I know a man who gave up smoking,
drinking, sex, and rich food. He was
healthy right up to the time he killed
himself.

Johnny Carson

Middle age is when your clothes no longer fit, and it's you who need the alterations.
Earl Wilson

It takes a long while to grow young.
Pablo Picasso

I think you can destroy your now by worrying about tomorrow.
Janis Joplin

The best way to grow old is not to be in a hurry about it.

At my age, I don't even buy green bananas.
Congressman Claude Pepper, at age 87

The secret of staying young is to live honestly, eat slowly, and lie about your age.
Lucille Ball

A sure sign of middle age is that, although we love seeing a "10" on the beach, we're willing to settle for two "5's."

Fred Shoenberg

If the young knew!—if the old could!

Alois Verre

If a young or middle-aged man does not
recollect where he laid his hat, it is
nothing; but if the same inattention is
discovered in an old man, people will
shrug their shoulders and say, "His
memory is going."

Samuel Johnson

Old people like to give good advice, since
they can no longer set bad examples.

La Rochefoucauld

I stopped a middle-aged person in the
street and asked, "Do you think mid-life
crisis is a consequence of ignorance or
apathy?" His answer: "I don't know and I
don't care."

Fred Shoenberg

Old age is like underwear: it creeps up on you.

Man is old when he begins to hide his age; woman, when she begins to tell hers.

Oscar Wilde

Young people tell what they are doing, old people what they have done, and fools what they wish to do.

French Proverb

You know you're getting older when you look forward to a dull evening.

Old age is like everything else. To make a success of it, you've got to start young.

Fred Astaire

Wrinkles are ditches that the gods have dug for our tears.

Emile Augier

You know you're getting older when
"scoring" has to do with shuffleboard.

Middle age is when you have a choice of two temptations and choose the one that will get you home earlier.

I must be getting absent-minded. Whenever I complain that things aren't what they used to be, I always forget to include myself.

George Burns

Old age lends poignancy to the saying, "If at first you don't succeed, try, try again."

You know you're getting older when getting lucky means you've won the lottery.

To me, old age is fifteen years older than I am.

Bernard M. Baruch

Old age is when candlelit tables are no longer romantic because you can't read the menu.

One should never trust a woman who tells one her real age. A woman who would tell that would tell anything.

Oscar Wilde

The young feel tired at the end of an action; The old at the beginning.

T.S. Eliot

If you wish to live long you must be willing to grow old.

George Lawton

We're recycling ourselves. Young people didn't invent activism. We were active in our day in the peace movement, the labor movement, the cooperative movement. The young seem to feel that old people descended from outer space. They forget we have a past.

Doris Mendez, Gray Panthers

You know you're getting older when a
matinee takes place in a theater.

What we do for ourselves dies with us;
what we do for others and the world
remains and is immortal.

Albert Pine

Well enough for old folks to rise early,
because they have done so many mean
things all their lives they can't sleep
anyhow.

Mark Twain

I don't admit age. I call it ripening. Like
all of nature, we are transformed into
future seed. Ripening has distinct
advantages for women—they have a
chance to regain their full identity as a
person.

Meridel Le Sueur, at age 84

Oh, to be seventy again!
Chief Justice Oliver Wendell Holmes, Jr.,
age 86, as a pretty girl passed by.

18

Growing old gracefully sure beats dying
with dignity.

Martha Holland Bartsch

The problem is that when you get it,
you're too damned old to do anything
about it.

Jimmy Connors, on experience

The older I grow the more I distrust the
familiar doctrine that age brings wisdom.

H. L. Mencken

The dead bird does not leave the nest.

Winston Churchill, on being advised
that his fly was open.

Old age is the most unexpected of all the
things that happen to a man.

Leon Trotsky

It is a man's own fault, it is from want of
use, if his mind grows torpid in old age.

Samuel Johnson

When you're over the hill, you pick up speed.

Bumper sticker: Money won't buy you happiness, but it keeps you in touch with your children.

Young men think old men are fools, but old men know young men are fools.

George Chapman

An old man continues to be young in two things—love of money and love of life.

Proverb

Wish not so much to live long as to live well.

Proverb

One should never make one's début with a scandal; one should reserve that to give interest to one's old age.

Oscar Wilde

Twenty years of romance make a woman
look like a ruin, but twenty years of
marriage make her something like a
public building.

Oscar Wilde

Young men want to be faithful and are not, old men want to be faithless and cannot.

Oscar Wilde

"She'll never admit it, but I believe it is Mama."

Zsa Zsa Gabor, when asked which Gabor was the oldest

Teach your children in youth, and they will not teach you in old age.

Hasidic Saying

There is no medicine against old age.

Nigerian Proverb

The young man knows the rules but the old man knows the exceptions.

Oliver Wendell Holmes

There was an Old Man with a beard,
Who said: "It is just as I feared!
  Two owls and a hen,
  Four larks and a wren
Have all built their nests in my beard."

Edward Lear

I am not young enough to know everything.

Oscar Wilde

Life has got to be lived—that's all there is to it. At seventy, I would say the advantage is that you take life more calmly. You know that 'this, too, shall pass!'

Eleanor Roosevelt

We are always the same age inside.

Gertrude Stein

Pick the right grandparents, don't eat or drink too much, be circumspect in all things, and take a two-mile walk every morning before breakfast.

Harry S Truman,
on how to reach the age of 80

When you're young, you want to be
master of your fate and captain of your
soul. When you're older, you'll settle for
being master of your weight and captain
of your bowling team.

George Roberts

Life's a tough proposition but the first
hundred years are the hardest.

Wilson Mizner

The denunciation of the young is a
necessary part of the hygiene of older
people, and greatly assists the circulation
of their blood.

Logan Pearsall Smith

All say, "How hard it is that we have to
die"—a strange complaint to come from
the mouths of people who have had to
live.

Mark Twain

The only two things we do with greater
frequency in middle age are urinate and
attend funerals.

Fred Shoenberg

An eccentric old spinster named Lowell
Announced to her friends, "Bless my sowell,
   I've gained so much weight
   I am sorry to state
I fear that I'm going to fowell."

Middle age starts the morning you get up, go to the bathroom, look in the mirror and admit that you are who you are going to be.

Fred Shoenberg

Middle age is nature's way of showing a sense of humor.

Fred Shoenberg

Old age is a shipwreck.

Charles De Gaulle

I find as I grow older that I love those most whom I loved first.

Thomas Jefferson

You're not as young as you used to be. But you're not as old as you're going to be. So watch it!

Irish Toast

A man of fifty looks as old as Santa Claus
to a girl of twenty.

William Feather

A FINE OLD MAN

John Wagner, the oldest man in Buffalo—one hundred and four years old—recently walked a mile and a half in two weeks.

He is as cheerful and bright as any of these other old men that charge around so persistently and tiresomely in the newspapers, and in every way as remarkable.

Last November he walked five blocks in a rainstorm, without any shelter but an umbrella, and cast his vote for Grant, remarking that he had voted for forty-seven presidents—which was a lie.

His "second crop" of rich brown hair arrived from New York yesterday, and he has a new set of teeth coming—from Philadelphia.

He is to be married next week to a girl one hundred and two years old, who still takes in washing.

They have been engaged eighty years, but their parents persistently refused their consent until three days ago.

John Wagner is two years older than the Rhode Island veteran, and yet has never tasted a drop of liquor in his life—unless—unless you count whisky.

Mark Twain

You know you're getting older when a
fortune teller offers to read your face.

Bumper sticker on RV: Mom and Dad's last toy.

How can they say my life isn't a success? Have I not for more than sixty years got enough to eat and escaped being eaten?
Logan Pearsall Smith

You know you're getting older when you order stewed prunes and the waiter says "excellent choice."

I can't imagine a wise old person who can't laugh.
Erik H. Erikson

Do not resist growing old—
Many are denied the privilege!
Irish Toast

Old age is when you go on a protest
march because you need the exercise.

Man is young as long as he can repeat his emotions; woman, as long as she can inspire them.

Oscar Wilde

Each person is born to one possession which outvalues all his others—his last breath.

Mark Twain

You do not teach the paths of the forest to an old gorilla.

African Proverb

Growing old is no more than a bad habit which a busy man has no time to form.

André Maurois

Old Boys have their Playthings as well as young Ones; the Difference is only in the Price.

Ben Franklin

In Summer he said she was fair,
In Autumn her charms were still there;
   But he said to his wife
   In the Winter of life
"There's no Spring in your old *derrière.*"

Jenny kissed me when we met,
Jumping from the chair she sat in;
Time, you thief, who love to get
Sweets into your list, put that in:
Say I'm weary, say I'm sad,
Say that health and wealth have missed me,
Say I'm growing old, but add,
Jenny kissed me.

Leigh Hunt

Grow old along with me!
The best is yet to be,
The last of life, for which the first was
    made.
Our times are in his hand.

Robert Browning

"You are old, Father William," the young
    man said,
"And your hair has become very white;
And yet you incessantly stand on your
    head—
Do you think, at your age, it is right?"

Lewis Carroll

They say such nice things about people at their funerals that it makes me sad to realize that I'm going to miss mine by just a few days.

Garrison Keillor

Golfer's prayer: May I live long enough to shoot my age.

A graceful and honorable old age is the childhood of immortality.

Pindar

I'm at the age where food has taken the place of sex in my life. In fact, I've just had a mirror put over my kitchen table.

Rodney Dangerfield

He who laughs lasts.

You know you're getting older when you wake up with that morning after feeling and you didn't do anything the night before.

Bumper sticker: If I'd known how
wonderful it would be to have
grandchildren, I'd have had them first.

I advise you to go on living solely to enrage those who are paying your annuities. It is the only pleasure I have left.

Voltaire

"Your money or your life."
"Take my life. I'm saving my money for my old age."

Irish Humor

Aging gracefully is for Baryshnikov.

Bill Cosby

It was the first time in my whole life that I realized my mother had a little girl down there inside her. And she taught me something that night: *There is no such thing as an old woman! We've been conned.* My [plastic surgery] patients are not vain. They only want to let the little girl out!

Dr. Harvey Austin, plastic surgeon

I smoke cigars because at my age if I don't
have something to hang onto I might fall
down.

George Burns

Most men employ the first years of their life in making the last miserable.

Jean de la Bruyère

That sign of old age, extolling the past at the expense of the present.

Sydney Smith

Young I was, but now am old,
But I am not yet grown cold;
I can play, and I can twine
'Bout a virgin like a vine:
In her lap too I can lie
Melting, and in fancy die:
And return to life, if she
Claps my cheek, or kisseth me;
Thus, and thus it now appears
That our love outlasts our years.

Robert Herrick

The fear of old age disturbs us, yet we are not certain of becoming old.

Jean de la Bruyère

Middle age: when you're sitting at home
on Saturday night and the telephone rings
and you hope it isn't for you.

Ogden Nash

I inhabit a weak, frail, decayed tenement;
battered by the winds and broken in upon
by the storms, and, from all I can learn,
the landlord does not intend to repair.
John Quincy Adams, after suffering a stroke

"I don't mind losing my locket," said the
mugging victim to the policeman, "but it
contained a lock of my husband's late
hair."

A person is always startled when he hears
himself seriously called an old man for
the first time.

Oliver Wendell Holmes

Time and trouble will tame an advanced
young woman, but an advanced old
woman is uncontrollable by any earthly
force.

Dorothy L. Sayers

You know you're old when you notice
how young the derelicts are getting.
Jeanne Phillips

The evening of a well spent life brings its lamps with it.

Joseph Joubert

Advice of old men is as the sun in Winter; it enlightens without warming.

Marquis de Vauvenargues

A Cato twenty years of age, an Adonis fifty years of age, are equally ridiculous.

Comte de Segur

It is perhaps the most demoralizing moment that a middle-aged man can know, even worse than learning that his twenty-six-year-old son is about to move back into the house or that his high school sweetheart has applied for membership in the Gray Panthers.

Bill Cosby, on failure
of short-term memory

No woman should ever be quite accurate
about her age. It looks so calculating.

Oscar Wilde

Middle age is the time when a man is always thinking that in a week or two he will feel as good as ever.

Don Marquis

As you get older, you get a little more magnanimous toward people who say things you despise.

Billy Wilder, at age 82

Experts agree that the elderly are usually not "losing it," they are just not "using it" as often.

Dr. Alvin F. Poussaint

First you forget names, then you forget faces, then you forget to pull your zipper up, then you forget to pull your zipper down.

Leo Rosenberg

You know you're getting older when you can't get your rocking chair started.

Age isn't important unless you're cheese.

For the unlearned, old age is winter; for the learned, it is the season of the harvest.

Hasidic Saying

Bumper sticker: We don't drink and drive. Our kids always have the car.

It's boring for a 71-year-old broad to sing about how bad she wants it, even if it is true we frequently want it badly.

Lena Horne

Said an eighty-year bridegroom named
Carr,
"My libido's too high, Doc, by far;
    But it's all in my head,
    Move it down here instead,
For I'd still like to be a papa."

A seventyish wife came home to find her husband making love to a neighbor. Furious, she slapped him; he lost his balance and rolled down the stairs. The family doctor phoned her to ask why she'd hit her husband—the poor guy had suffered a sprained shoulder. "Well, Doc," she said, "if he can do what he did at seventy-five, I figured he could fly."

The Tonight Show

I am not afraid of tomorrow, for I have seen yesterday and I love today.

William Allen White

"Don't worry about senility," my grandfather used to say. "When it hits you, you won't know it."

Bill Cosby

Youth is in the mind, not in the condition of your flesh.

Ginger Rogers

Wrinkles should merely indicate where
the smiles have been.

Mark Twain

There are three faithful friends—an old wife, an old dog, and ready money.

Benjamin Franklin

Nature is full of freaks, and now puts an old head on young shoulders, and then a young heart beating under fourscore winters.

Ralph Waldo Emerson

The only good thing about the decline of my memory is that it has brought me closer to my mother, for she and I now forget everything at the same time.

Bill Cosby

Men may become old, but they never become good.

Oscar Wilde

Excuse my dust.

Dorothy Parker,
suggestion for her own epitaph

I'm not a magician. I can't make you young again.

Konrad Adenauer's physician,
treating him for a cold when
Adenauer was 90 years old.

I haven't asked you to. All I want is to go on getting older.

Konrad Adenauer

So, lively brisk old fellow, don't let age get you down. White hairs or not, you can still be a lover.

Goethe

They who would be young when they are old, must act old when they are young.

Proverb

We do not count a man's years until he has nothing else to count.

Ralph Waldo Emerson

You know you're getting older when
Medicare will pick up 80% of the cost of
the honeymoon.

There is a vast difference between success at twenty-five and success at sixty. At sixty, nobody envies you. Instead, everybody rejoices generously, sincerely, in your good fortune.

Marie Dressler

I don't see why not, young man. You look reasonably fit to me.

Winston Churchill, to a photographer photographing him on his 80th birthday, who expressed the wish to photograph him again on Churchill's 100th birthday.

One trouble with growing older is that it gets progressively tougher to find a famous historical figure who didn't amount to much when he was your age.

Bill Vaughan

Age before beauty.

Clare Boothe Luce

Pearls before swine.

Dorothy Parker

Certain connections just seem to be
beyond me at this age. For example, if
someone calls me on the telephone and
says, "Can you meet me at the Seven-
Eleven at eight?" I show up at the Five-
and-Ten at nine.

Bill Cosby

A retired husband is a wife's full-time job.

I wake up every morning at nine and grab for the morning paper. Then I look at the obituary page. If my name is not on it, I get up.

Harry Hershfield

There was an old spinster from Fife,
Who had never been kissed in her life;
   Along came a cat,
   And she said "I'll kiss that!"
But the cat meowed: "Not on your life!"

Growing old isn't so bad if you consider the alternative.

Why is it that at class reunions you feel
younger than everyone else looks?

If I'd known I was gonna live this long, I'd
have taken better care of myself.

Eubie Blake, at age 100